A DIET OF POEMS IN A
SLIM VOLUME

KT-369-161

FOREWORD

This book of poems has been published as a 50th birthday surprise for the author, so he has not had the opportunity to make any fine edits or changes to his poems. However, he has only himself to blame because we in the family have been trying to get him to do this for years, but Russell being Russell has avoided the issue with mumblings about "vanity publishing".

Apart from one or two poems that have been selected for printing when he entered them for poetry competitions the public at large have not had the opportunity to share in the enjoyment that we have had for many years from Russell's work, so if he won't publish we must. Of course it would be equivocal to suggest that our motives are entirely altruistic because, although we have been pinching copies of individual poems for years, none of us till now have had a proper set covering the wide range over which Russell wanders when he sits down to commit his thoughts to paper. Although this may appear to be a present for Russell, it is really a present for ourselves and hopefully it will encourage him to continue to provide us with further enjoyment for many years to come and we don't have to wait another 50 years for a second volume.

Any doubts there may have been about a wider audience appreciating these poems were quickly dispelled when this collection was revealed to the various people who needed to be involved in bringing this project to truition. One of them, Dee Brady, who typed the initial format had her husband coming up stairs to find out why she was sitting at her word processor chuckling away to herself-and she is a Birmingham lass! So although there is a underlying Scottish influence through the work, it is now known that this book will travel well across borders.

At this point in forewords it is usual to name those who helped make this publication possible and Geoff Cadman of Inprint Services falls into this category, both for his technical help and cost minimising assistance, but the others can only really be identified as conspirators. The chief conspirators are my wife Margaret who conceived the idea and Russell's wife Freda who acquired most of the original works unknown to the author. In addition there are all the other family members and friends who pre-ordered copies to make the venture financially possible.

Anyone who has read these poems so far has almost invariably found at least one with which they can personally identify and I am sure this will be the case for all future readers. Initially we thought of putting the poems into chapters with a common theme but the subject matter is so diverse it put that idea into the "too difficult" category so the random order means that you can open the book anywhere and delve in not knowing what to expect next and join us in the secret pleasure we have had to ourselves so far.

Warwick Adams
May 1998

Contents

Here's a wee book o' poems
Ah hope ye will enjoy
An' get many hoors o' pleasure
Both to man and boy.
Ah read it masel', it's really good
Ah say that from the heart
But Ah'll no write doon any mair
So's ye can make a start.

Written on the fly leaf of a book of other
peoples' poems given as a present in 1985

———————◆◆◆———————

A HEART TO PUMP TALK

My illusions were shattered,
When I saw in a dictionary
My heart was a pump.
I rushed home for a pump to pump talk
With my sweetpump.
She was pumpbroken.
It had muscled in on our love.
She said it didn't matter,
Our love was not in vein.
- Her pump's in the right place.

DEAD GIVEAWAY

Stitching time at the mortuary
On a body split apart.
A busy doctor rushes in
"Quick, I need a heart!"
"Sorry, gone to Papworth,
We only had the one."
"Never mind", says the doctor,
"Could you let me have a lung?"
"Sorry, gone to smoking research."
The doctor says, "Well, I never!
Still - while I've done a scrub-up
Could you let me have a liver?"
"Sorry, it's been transplanted
Into a man who came from Sydney.
Before you ask, he'd a donor card
So they also took his kidney!"
"What about his - er, twiddley bits?"
"They've been deposited in a bank,
As sperm for test tube babies
You've new research to thank."
"Eyes?" "A cataract operation."
"What about his brain?"
"It's being dissected on TV
In a medical panel game!"
The frustrated surgeon gave a sigh,
He was becoming quite demented.
He grabbed the body - rushed out saying,
"There's maybe money back on the empties!"

"Who was that masked man?"

Des Res (View by Appointment)

My frnd mrrd an estate agnt
Nd hw hr lfe hs chngd
We only gt to see hr
If it's prvsly arrngd.
So if we pop in cassly
Nd she dsn't kno wr cming
Shll shw us al hr pwr points
Nd lt us see the plming.
Thy lve in a lttle des res
2 mnts frm the sea
Tht's if you fly n Cncrde
Nd py a survyrs fee.
Hr lfs abbrviatd
She sys tht suts hr fine
Thy mk love in two mnts
Nd stll hve tme to dine.
She hs all hr fixtres nd fttngs
Shs nvr evr phasd
Nd talk of cntrl htng
Mks hr eyes go dble glzd.
Bt wht of the futr
If thr ardr strts to pale
Wll I see hr in the grdn
Wth a sign tht sys FR SALE.

WORLD WAR 2 EPISODE 19

World War 2 was old Newsreels
The Pathé Pictorial to victory,
With clipped voiced jingoism
Overdubbing the death throes
Of a civilisation

Where grey soldiers fought in
Thinning uniformed rows
And grey tanks rumbled mercilessly
Over shattered grey landscapes
Crushing the dreams

Sullen black eyes staring sadly
From broken villages and towns
Voices unheard on the soundtrack
But barbed wire enclosures
Spoke for themselves

And grey battleships throwing puffs of smoke
At aeroplanes diving to kill
With black hunters in the ocean beneath them
Waiting to pounce
In the name of glory

And so the grey images kept running
Filling up can after can
To haunt the minds of filmgoers
A black and white war filmed on a huge set
But the blood was red.

━━━━━━✦✦✦━━━━━━

COCCYX

Where your bot sits
That's your coccyx
If it was any lower
It would be covered by your soccyx

HALF NELSON

"Horatio! Please don't go!"
Lady Hamilton bleated.
"When you're overseas
Your faculties
Are being continually depleted.
Why must you sail
Where wars prevail?"
She asked him, rather quizzically.
"It means I'm seeing less of you.
Both metaphorically -
And Physically!"

Nelson winked his one good eye.
Hugged her with his arm.
"Be strong my love,
For God above
Will spare me further harm.
It's part of some great master plan
In which we mortals fit
God wants me up in heaven so
He's taking me bit by bit."

———————◆◆◆———————

STAGE STRUCK

No amateur this who struts the stage
With consummate ease
But a seasoned professional
Steeped in tradition
With natural instinct
Skilled beyond his years.
Plumbing the depths of every scene,
Subtly playing on each emotion
Entertaining us, draining us,
Wringing us dry with his tears.
Having given his all the audience succumbs
He reaps his just rewards
Our four-year-old gets to stay up late
This master of the boards.

DOING THE DISHES

Festering like blisters
On rooftops and buildings
Silent white spheres
Staring up at the sky.
Unseen transmissions
Beamed through the airwaves
Flooding small rooms
In the wink of an eye.
Proud owners clockwatch
This non-stop bonanza
Images paraded
Saturating their screens
They sit there not stirring
Constantly watching
Their lives are lived for them
By satellite beams.

—————✦✦✦—————

THE BULLY

He liked to annoy the little boys
Spoil their games and break their toys,
Steal their biscuits from their lunch
And laugh at them as he went munch!
He also bullied little girls,
Broke their pencils, pulled their curls
When it rained he splashed them all with water,
And did other things he didn't oughter!
Like putting worms into their wellies
And calling them weeds, and wimps, and smelly!
No one liked him for doing that,
He really was a loathsome brat.
Then one day he gave a groan
No one would play - he was left alone.
It didn't matter he tried to make amends
He found he didn't have any friends.

Taking My Medicine

I was extremely fortunate
The only person in my street
Six lucky numbers alone were mine
The Readers Digest monthly treat.
To show my undying gratitude
I invested in their latest tome
But since my medical book arrived
I've been too ill to leave my home.
From being the very picture of health
Fit, and well, and in my prime
Every page I start to read
I have the symptoms every time.
I had Angina by chapter one
Anaemia and Autism as well
Cirrhosis, Colitis by chapter three
And other things I cannot spell.
For every twitch and every itch
I look it up, I know its name
Dengue fever, Croup and Impetigo
Without them life is not the same.
My blood and heart, my bones and joints,
My glands, my cells, my perspiration
Are wracked by Typhus, Anthrax, Yaws
Lassa Fever and Inflammation.
I get the sweats and palpitations
Every time I cough and sneeze
I'm sure I'm coming down again
With some rare tropical disease.
My only hope of some salvation
While this pain my soul endures
Is that the Digests next great offer
Will be sending me a book of cures

How About Some Shakespeare Shorts

Hamlet

Someone killed my dad
And it drove me mad.

Romeo And Juliet

I love you madly
Let's go tell the family.

Julius Caesar

The Emperor's home
No more to Rome.

King Lear

It's choppy waters
Trying to please your daughters.

Macbeth

If you want my crown
Go chop a forest down.

Merchant Of Venice

It's fine to bet
Make sure you get your cut.

GREAT MOMENTS IN HISTORY PART 1 - PRESUMABLY

Deep in darkest Africa
Livingstone realised to his cost
The last thing he'd discovered was
He'd found out he was lost.
He'd been busily converting natives
As missionaries often did
With mirrors, beads and trinkets
And a cheque for fifty quid.
While back in civilisation
An ageing tabloid hack
Said, "I will go to Africa
And bring the great man back."
This brave soul was Stanley
To whom Livingstone owed his life,
Noted then for tracking skills
And not his sharp blade knife
Which he used to hack down creepers
Swathed a path to a village hut
Helped by a pygmy barber
Who'd pointed out a shortcut.
"Dr Livingstone I presume."
His words sliced through the air
And the village chief said "Not me you fool
That's him over there!"
And so the two great men embraced
Beneath the jungle dome
Then Stanley said his famous words
"How the hell do I get home?"

WEDDING HATS

With an ostrich expired and perched on her head,
The Bride's mother sits at the end of a pew,
Next to a lampshade that would be right at home,
In the lighting department inside B and Q.
A pile of pancakes perched at an angle,
Joins another concoction seen on parade,
With black feathers splaying in several directions.
Like a crow that's swallowed a hand grenade.
And some strawberry netting pinned to a sweet bag,
Seen as the height of the milliner's art,
Is displayed by an Auntie who wore it not thinking,
A fool and her money are soon prised apart.
A flying saucer, an upside down Wok
A Pill Box and a second hand turban
Statements of fashion riddle the church
Haute couture, yet quaintly suburban.
A demented racoon, a candy floss bonnet,
These arty confections are worn with some pride,
Posing for photo's and hogging the video
Desperately trying to outdo the bride.
The vicar looks on with a glazed-faced expression
The thought of a wedding just fills him with dread
At the thought of all the lady guests invited
Who let the occasion go straight to their head

DIGESTIVE SYSTEMS

Your digestive system
Is very interintestine
It stretches half the length
Of a football pitch
But will it bring the crowds back
Or curb soccer violence?

THE NEW RELIGION

A few old people littered the church
Clinging to pews for insurance purposes
While the new religion
Prospered across the street.
In the latest purpose built, mega sized
Open 365 days a year
Betta Builda DIY centre
The church of the Latter Day Paints
Worshippers come in their hundreds.
8 to 8 every Sunday
Including Christmas.
Aisles not filled with meditation
But shoppers consulting lists
Notebooks of measurements
With thinking only as deep
As the foundations of their new patio
Tills ring out in joyous exultation
Summoning the throng
To worship at the new built alter
Salvation is cheaper here
Or the difference refunded
If there were to be a second coming
The people would not be found
In some ageing stone faced edifice
Chained to their history
But thronged in their thousands
Clutching louvered doors
Waiting to be converted
The only consolation being
This time
The nails and wood are handy.

Ballad Of Four Folk Singers

Take your finger from your ear
Fold your Arran for the day.
Put your banjo in its case,
Let the notes no longer play.
Unstrung guitars are quiet now,
Their tunes are gone in dotted lines.
The younger singers moving in,
A sign of the wild and mountain thymes.
Liverpool's left for evermore,
The Judies scattered are - and fled.
The hills no more are roved upon,
The battles fought are slain and dead.
The four folk singers sit in gloom,
Their ashes scattered on the sea.
Their ballads fall on empty rooms
And rest some where 'twixt time and me.

Blackpool

Plastic-mac mums, clutching kids at right angles
Descend to the sands with their buckets and spades
Till conspiring winds drive them across tired tram-tracks
Into the jaws of the penny arcades.
While up in the tower the organ is sounding
To the echo of dance steps from ages gone by
And people protesting have emptied the circus
Children haunt funfairs manufactured nearby.
Moth-eaten donkeys tread squares on the beach
Side shows and slot machines have invaded the pier.
But dress it all up in lights and nostalgia
And back come the trippers, year after year

EVENTIDE OLD FOLKS HOME

They sit in their armchairs
With jelly like chins.
And nodding-dog heads.
Talking in a time-warp
About long ago wars.
Knitting their lives to their end.
They sleep through the TV
Lives remote from their own
With some snatched conversation
Staying still on their lips.
Glass eyes scan obituaries,
Saying goodbye to their friends.
Their memories are crowded
With never ending sunshine.
Rose coloured concoctions
Of times now passed by.
As their bodies complain
And slowly submit to
The idea of being old.
Sympathetic servants
Feed them and clothe them
And mentally approach them
With "Do not disturb" signs.
But here they have friendship
And her they have safety
In each others ageing.
Their life sung round a piano,
Keeping them warm
Till the fires grow cold.

A Salesman Came Calling

A knock on the door "how do you do.
I am a salesman from up at the zoo.
They're closing it down, so we've animals to spare
I can sell you a zebra, a yak or a bear".

He offered an ostrich. "It's expired" I said.
"It's stunned." he explained "It's not really dead.
A car backfired as we walked up the street
And it tried to bury its head in the concrete."

"A comatose ostrich around here is rare.
They are quieter than dogs and don't leave a hair.
A conversation piece when neighbours abound
And one egg each morning is enough to go round."

I politely declined. The man started cryin'.
"In that case," he sobbed "can I sell you a lion."
"Does it like children?" I asked quite discrete.
"It does," he replied "but it prefers lumps of meat."

I said no to the lion - for the time being at least.
The supermarket had run out of fresh wildebeest.
An elephant? No. I couldn't come to terms
With sharing my house with some sad pachyderms.

He tried selling monkeys and wolves that were grey.
"You can make a deposit." I said "Yes so can they!"
I was getting annoyed. "This nonsense must cease.
If you don't go away I will call the Police."

He turned and went though his face showed the pain.
I closed the door but the bell rang again.
There stood the man "Have you phoned the Police station?
I was wondering if the sergeant would buy an Alsation!

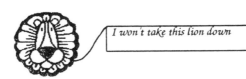

I won't take this lion down

ATTILA THE DUNN

While underneath a hypnotic trance
To allow his boils to be lanced
To his amazement Mr Dunn
Discovered he was Attila the Hun
In a previous life, in a bygone age,
He'd been the leader who was all the rage.
So now he's the menace of the village
Going out to steal and pillage
With his friend Bert a lonely man
Who once thought he was Gengis Khan.
But being a despot is quite risky
When you're fat, and bald, and over sixty!
His patient wife - one Mrs Dunn
Found life hard as Mrs Hun
For every morning before she'd rise
He'd have a ritual sacrifice.
It's no fun trying to have a sleep
In a bedroom full of dismembered sheep.
The mess he made was an affront
And it made her breadknife very blunt.
So despairingly she flew the nest
While Attila beat his hairy chest
Which he kept in a cupboard underneath
His wig, false eye, and set of teeth.
He'd set off with his hairy hoard
The bus driver wouldn't let him board
It was in a regulation
Marauding hordes stayed in the station
So sad, despondent beyond measure
He realised there was no pleasure.
To the hypnotist returned Mr Dunn
To see if he's been Napoleon!

I've lost my bus pass as well

THE AUCHENTOGGLE BURNS NIGHT

'Twas in the depths of January
When the sna' wis blawin' hard,
The kilts and haggis dusted off
Tae toast the National Bard.
The tartan plaids and satin frocks
Shivered into a dim lit room
An' cursed at Rab for no bein' born
In the warmth filled days o' sunny June.

The Auchentoggle businessmen
Whose annual do this supper was
Were gettin' hot and bothered an'
Their erstwhile chairman wis the cause
He wis a Chinese restaurateur
A Mr Hi Lan Way
Who'd never heard o' Rabbie Burns
And didn't know whit tae dae.

So, instead o' haein haggis there
To say the Selkirk Grace
They'd a plate o' crispy noodles
Served up to take its place.
Of a' the words that Rabbie wrote
And he had much to say,
He never waxed in lyric form
Aboot a Chinese take-away.

The piper heralded the feast
His chanter giving forth a lilt
But he played an extra grace note when
The wind blew gently up his kilt.
The steaming repast set in place
Up stood Mr Hi Lan Way
Not used to old John Barleycorn,
He wis hot an' steamin' tae.

"Gleat chieftain o' la pluddin lace"
The room was bathed in eerie quiet.
Mrs Way had taen offence
For she'd been strictly oan a diet.
This trial oer they a' tucked in
To loads o' noodles, neeps and nips,
Throwin' it doon their throats at speed
Wi' hardly time tae touch their lips.

The Immortal Memory cam' next
The life an' works o' Rab tae toast
Eck Smith uttering words profound
He'd borrowed from the Sunday Post.
Eck wis the local slaughterman,
A president o' the future
He spoke for over half an hour
Oan the trials o' bein' a butcher.

O' choppin' up died coos an' lambs
O' a' the pigs he'd gi'en their knell.
Then he rendered "To a Mouse"
An' slowly murdered that as well.
Milkman Mac was next tae rise
A' present raised tae him their glasses
This agin' Romeo hid the task
O' toastin' a' the bonnie lassies.

He spoke o' empathy wi' Rab
How lovin' wimmin' made life hard.
Bein' banned fae hooses a' ower the place
He wis called the Immortal Barred
Old spinster Murphy heard his words
An' she wis just too shocked tae speak.
She made her mind up there an' then,
Tae order extra milk next week.

Tae reply rose Maggie Henderson
A charmin' lass soon tae be weddin'
Eyebrows raised and comments hushed
As a' observed her figure spreadin'
She thanked Mac fir his eloquence
The air was filled wi' warm romance
She added that the lump was his
An' she'd be wantin' maintenance.

Mac sat rooted tae his chair
Seein' this lass he'd like tae throttle
Afraid tae speak or dae a thing
A milkman who hid lost his bottle.
The nips were flowin' fast and free
The spirits rose as spirits downed
Till a' wir bleezed in golden hue
An' pride and prejudice broke down.

A singin' voice broke through the haze,
Pure as is a baby's kiss
Meg Munro sang "Red Red Rose"
A well-endowed an' prim young miss.
"Till a' the seas gang dry, my dear
And the rocks melt wi' the sun!"
Straining to "luve thee still, my dear,"
Her heavin' bodice came undone.

"An' fare the weel my only luve,
An' fare thee weel a while."
She made a beeline oot the ha'
"Tho' it were ten thousand mile.
Rab would be richt overjoyed
True great wid' be his measure
To see this renderin o' his sang
Gie so mony folk sic pleasure.

The dancers set to oan the flair
An eightsome wis the chairman's pick
Wheelin' roon in develish glee
Till nearly everyone wis sick.
A Dashing White Sargeant followed on,
They drapped aroon' the room like flies
Auld Tam slipped an' did the splits
Tears o' happiness filled his eyes.

Four braw lads wi' kilts an' dirks
Did a sword dance quick an' flash
Wan slipped an' severed half his toe
He could really cut a dash.
He did his own wee heilan' fling
His antics wir pathetic.
A plaster stemmed the flow o' blood
Wi' whisky fir an anasthetic.

So tae the high spot o' the night
An' end tae dance an' banter.
Fyffe McPherson filled the stage
Ready to deliver Tam O' Shanter
A seasoned supperite he stands and waits
The rabble hush to hear him utter
Rab's immortal ode tae Tam
It's a pity Fyffe speaks wi' a stutter

He launches forth intae the poem
His diction right, his tone complete.
But Chapman Billies need half an 'oor,
Before they leave the street.
He struggles on in rich broad voice
It really seems an awfy shame,
By the time he sees Kirk Alloway
The witches an' warlocks hiv' a' gone hame.

Their cleekin' and clackin' wis a' done,
By the time poor Maggie's at the brig
The immortal punters are at the bar
Tryin' tae hae a last wee swig.
Finally, - tae Auld Lang Syne
Linkin' arms an' staunin' roon,
Haudin' each ithers airms fir luck
An' tae stop each ither fain' doon.

Wi' misty eyes an' misty breath
They a' crowd in an' shed a tear
Then pit awa' their Burns an' thoughts
Till they can dust them doon next year.

CRISP BAGS IN THE PLAYGROUND

Why me? Was I the nearest one?
As the crisp bags dance in the breeze.
Sentenced to go an pick them up,
And without so much as a "Please".
You don't know where the playground's been,
I might catch a disease.
Salt and Vinegar, Smokey Bacon,
Tasty fries and Mini Chips
A thousand bags, a thousand flavours,
Crunched between a thousand lips.
Now this bag here, it might be special,
Sonya Binns of 7B
Might have held it, crunched crisps from it,
Left it lying just for me.
She lent me a pencil sharpener
When my own was broken.
A mutual bond on a sharpened point,
Though never a word was spoken.
I'll take it home and iron it flat,
Keep it always near my heart.
Me and Sonya's Barbecue Beef
We will never part.
But second thoughts, there's lots of bags here,
Discarded and alone.

A POSTCARD HOME

Hello folks, wish you were here,
Having a lovely time.
Spent the day with new found friends
Here at junction 29.
Tomorrow, if the weather holds,
And of course we don't sleep late
All of us are moving on
Hoping to reach junction 28.

Feud for Thought

It all began at the village fete, one blissful sunny summer's day
When the vegetable judging had taken place,
The Mayor got up to have his say.
The rosette for first prize was pinned on Jethro's laden barrow.
Everyone had been and admired the large size of his marrow!

Old Tom was his rival - was he magnanimous in defeat?
Not on your life, he took out his knife and with a piercing cry of "CHEAT!"
Plunged it in Jed's marrow to end the Championships
In a burst of skin and flesh and juice and a mighty shower of pips.

Jethro grabbed a cucumber and bore down on Old Tom,
Who picked up a likewise vegetable and like two gunfighters at dawn,
They squared up to each other, across the runner beans,
And would have marinated each other if the police hadn't intervened.

"What's going on?", the Mayor enquired, as the constables prised them free.
"There's been dirty deeds afoot", said Tom. "Someone's stolen me recipe
For fertiliser I made afore the show. It never used to fail.
I'd mixed it up from manure I got - straight from the horse's tail."

"That proves I'm no cheat", said Jed. "I never stole your mixture.
When I'm at home, I grow me own. My onions are a fixture.
And there's another way to prove my innocence, of course.
This is just a one horse town and I own the only horse!"

Here We Go - Again

Like a Hollywood sequel the nightmare returns
The déja-vu of a minnow defeat.
Hopes at half mast and our tartan in tatters
When we should have had the world at our feet.
Is it a case of the poor getting stronger
Or more to the point, are we getting weaker?
Will Scotland progress in the Italian World Cup
Or be left behind counting the Old Costa Rica.

A CHIP OFF THE OLD BLOCK

I'm Antonio Morono the sculptor
An witha ma chisel am gonna
Carve from this 20 foot rock face
A statue of Chiid and Madonna
Chip, chip, chip, chip
Chip, chip, chip, CLUNK!

'Sno matter I makea da error
A great sculptor no makea da moan
I'll carve from this 15 foot rock face
A Madonna all on her own.
Chip, chip, chip, chip
Chip, chip, chip, CLUNK!

I makea some slight alterations
An da statue will be a complete
She's standing up in da water
So I no need to carvea da feet
Chip, chip, chip, chip
Chip, chip, chip, CLUNK!

I gotta alla de time in da world
No need to makea da haste
I'll wait untila de tide's in
An' carve her up to da waist
Chip, chip, chip, chip
Chip, chip, chip, CLUNK!

Antonio he's not a worried
Something I gotta adjust
From dis towering 3 foot a rock face
I carve a Madonna's a bust
Chip, chip, chip, chip
Chip, chip, chip, CLUNK!

So now I makea ma fortune
Ma plans am gonna unravel
For people building their houses
I'll sell them plenty of gravel
Chip, chip, chip, chip
Chip, chip, chip, CLUNK!

BET LYNCH'S BIRTHDAY

6000 episodes of Coronation Street have gone
And we've come to celebrate
The 90 candles Granny Bet Lynch has on
Her celebration cake
She'll reflect on a cobbled lifetime
The drama and the dark intrigue
And the kids who've never known a time
When Liverpool didn't win the league.
When Steve Davis wasn't on the box
And Champion of the world.
She'll sit and knit Old Alex socks
In a life that's plain and purled
And we who've shared these episodes
Will join in this event
Knowing like Bet we have survived
And switch off quite content.

THE ART OF CONVERSATION

I hung over fences on warm summer evenings
As labours were left and the world put to rights.
I was whispered sweet nothings on dark-spangled dance floors
Clandestine promises on soft moonlit nights.
I danced between families in bathrooms and bedrooms
Negotiating lifestyles for parents and young.
I was sipped with warm coffee in cafés while shopping
I was love on the phone while quiet songs were sung.
Now I'm under threat from loud disco musak
Invading the pubs and the clubs and the bars.
It haunts me while shopping - the noise never stopping
Machines in the houses and phones in the cars.
Overwhelmed by TV's, radios, stereos
Losing my battle, my fight to be heard.
Will people remember the art of conversing,
Or will the noise drown me and have the last word!

ALLY OOPS

Pride was Argentina
In 1978
Sat by the telly with a can or two
Well, perhaps it was nearer a crate.

We'd been all hyped up on Ally
A roller coaster that just wouldn't stop.
With all the tartan paraphernalia
Sold by his wife at the Co-op.

It was only a matter of counting
Goals - scored by the Boys In Blue
They would grace the pitch with their presence,
But nobody told Peru.

Still - a minor aberration
In our World Cup master plan
Back to the box with a beer or two
To watch us humble Iran.

So! These emergent footballing nations
Are improving all the time.
And Scotland managed a creditable draw
Was that really such a crime.

It was a bitter pill to swallow
A purgatory bordering on hell.
And Willie Jhonstone was soon jetting home
For swallowing things as well.

So don't cry for me Argentina
Like a lame man who'd mislaid his crutch
We staggered to certain oblivion
Against the total footballing Dutch.

Scotland won with a goal of pure magic,
Archie Gemmill, the genius who scored.
A shining gem in a World Cup of dross
So pride was a little restored.

Now for Scotland the glitter has ended.
We'd experienced new depths of pain
Our pride won't get hyped up ever again,
Or again, and again and again.

D. I. Why

Piece of wood - hammer - nail,
Hammer - thumb - mighty wail!
D. I. Cry.

Paste all lumpy, plumb line - scratch
Strip of paper - doesn't match!
D. I. Sigh.

Flat packed cupboard - comes in bits.
Plan of pieces - not one fits!
D. I. Lie.

Paint pots, paint cards - book of tips
Runny finish, brush hair - drips!
D. I. Try.

Tap needs fixing - washer dud.
Put in new one - mighty flood!
D. I. Mystify.

Gutter leaking - minutes to fix
Ladder collapses - in ward 6!
D. I. Petrify.

Landscaped garden - terraced layers
Finished project - Himalayas!
D. I. Horrify.

Appliance faulty - fuse in stock
Fix it in - nasty shock!
D. I. Electrify.

Convert a kitchen - little trouble
Retaining wall - pile of rubble!
D. I. Crucify.

If things need doing - have a plan
Keep phone handy - call in man.
D. I. Diversify.

THE REEL THING

The video annoyed him
Blinking incessantly
Silent, black
But accessible to everyone
Even the most unimaginative
Untrained mind
Could bring it to life
Instantly.

He longed for his old ciné
There was real filming
Craft, artistry
Cleverly combined
In an enduring family ritual
Where he was the centrepiece
Fumbling in ecstasy
Threading a snake of film
Through a veritable forest
Of cogs, wheels and
Pre-planned channels
That he alone knew about.
The putting up of the screen
Hurried closing of curtains
Heralded the visual treat
Invited viewers whispered
In reverent tones
As switching brought to life
Grainy images
Chaplinesque in their silent movement
Familiar, yet strange
As he voiced over
Till the tape flap, flap, flapped
Whipping itself to death
On the end of a whirring wheel.

No longer centre stage
He envied the video
Colourful, loud and instant
But lacking a sense of occasion.

Holiday Haircut

In brown knee-length shorts
And black plastic sandals
Dragged off to honour
Some strict annual contract
My Dad had with the Barber
(Short for barbarian)
The offending half crown
Saw me shorn like a sheep
Scalped to the bone
In best pudding-basin style
With a small tuft remaining
So Daddy could grab it
And if I offended
Give me a clip round the ear.

The Haggis Hunters

"It's Burns Night, it's Burns Night!"
The little haggis cried.
"Here come the Haggis Hunters,
We'll have to run and hid!"
So they scattered on the hillside,
The heather, and the rocks.
Anywhere that they could hide
And shiver in their socks.

"What's a Haggis Hunter Mum?"
A baby haggis asked.
"You're better not to know my dear,"
She said, as tear she masked.
Daddy haggis looked quite grim,
For he remembered when,
Old Angus went to fight these beasts
And was never seen again!

The tale is told of Angus
At the haggis highland games.
When they're finished Haggis Dancing,
And are seated round the flames.
How he fought the Haggis Hunters,
Called Cecil, Nigel, Fred
Who beat him with their silver spoons,
To make sure he was dead!

27

They put him in a heated pot
And stirred him roon an' roon.
Then they tried to deafen him,
By playing a bagpipe tune.
They further tried to torture him
By chanting out a rhyme
About chieftains o' the puddin' race,
Tim'rous beasties, and Auld Lang Syne.

Then they heard a mannie speak,
And a song about their granny.
By that time they'd fallen asleep
It really was uncanny, ·
For then at last old Angus struck,
The winner without question.
By turning bad inside their tums
He gave them indigestion!

So every January 25th.,
As the Haggis Hunters come
They remember Uncle Angus
And the feeling in their turn
They feel quite faint and dizzy,
And go straight home to bed.
Then toast the ghost o' Rabbie Burns
With Bread and cheese instead.

— ◆◆◆ —

THE ASHBOURNE HIGHLAND GAMES

They talk of Lornach, Kyle, Braemar,
And other famous names.
But in the South, one ranks with these
The Ashbourne Highland Games.

The tartan ranks come in their hordes
Across the Derbyshire hills,
To meet, compete, serve up a treat
And display their various skills.

Graceful dancers, pirouette
In a carefully timed routine
Hands and feet in symmetry
For that extra point to glean.

The skirl of pipes lies on the air
The drums rap·out their beat
The kilted bands look proud and grand
As for trophies they compete.

The heavies' muscles strain to throw
Great weights - their body toils
With cabers tossed - points won and lost
The winner takes the spoils.

Upon the hill the runners sprint
Keeping up a steady pace,
Lean and taut - with just one thought,
To be winner of the race.

Excited spectators, watch, support,
And have the odd glass of beer
While special events go on around
Adding to the atmosphere.

When the games are done, and trophies won,
There comes a special treat
As the bands together - to everyone's pleasure
Go marching through the street.

A highlight then - the Ashbourne Games,
Fills everyone with cheer.
Contestants leave and make a vow
They'll be back again next year.

A Modern Midfielder

He'd been given permission by his agent to play.
His hairdresser said his coiffure was OK.
His modelling contractors didn't mind at all
As long as he refrained from heading the ball
He was reasonably healthy, his fitness was par
His chauffeur had driven him there in his car
He'd promoted the club in the best way he can
Once even stopping to speak to a fan.
His boots were well polished, no sign of dirt
With his sponsors emblazoned on front of his shirt
He posed for the Press then strode on the pitch
His pre-match preparation had gone without hitch
He'd train in the morning, showing off to his peers
Then off to the disco for a couple of beers
But football traditions are bigger than players
Respects no reputations or how many shares
He might have in the club. As in games long ago
The ball hit his groin and laid the lad low.
As they stretchered him off still writhing in pain
The trainer remarked, "It's a funny old game!"

29

A Quiet Day

All was quiet, the heads were down,
Everyone was hard at work.
Then a bee flew in the window
And the whole place went berserk!
Girls ran screaming round the room,
As it buzzed and weaved about.
Boys grabbed rulers, rolled up jotters,
Flailing round to knock it out.
Sir's voice thundered, "Don't alarm it
Leave it alone - and away it goes."
He opened the window to let it out,
And it stung him on the nose!

Lest We Forget

"What's that up on the hill?"
"A monument."
"What's it for?"
"Can't remember."

BIG DEAL AT THE DOGS' HOME

The closing bell had tolled and the dogs, they weren't sold
The canines caged within looked near their end.
In the grip of a recession, the very first possession
That is surplus to the house, is man's best friend.

But hopes were raised on high, when a stranger entered nigh
He shouted out, "I need a dog, and quick!"
"You don't need to bawl, I've got doggies wall to wall",
Said the startled owner, "You can take your pick!"

"Do you want it for a pet, or even better yet
A large ferocious dog to guard your flat.
An Alsatian would be nice, you'd get lots of exercise
Especially if it ever saw your cat."

"No, no, said the caller, I was wanting something smaller
Big dewy eyes and lots of cuddly charms.
I don't care about the breed, a Chihuahua's all I need,
As long as I can hold it in my arms."

"Now let me get this straight, you only care about the weight
A pedigree is surplus to your wants!"
"Yes, I don't want any training, like walkies when it's raining
Or poopa scooping round its favourite haunts."

The owner, growing vexed, asked a might perplexed
"Your attitude quite frankly does appall.
You don't care about its breeding, its comfort or its feeding,
I don't think you want to have a dog at all!"

The customer went berserk, "It's the escalator at my work!
I need to travel up it - but I'm thwarted.
DOGS MUST BE CARRIED says the sign,
And for some folks that is fine,
But I haven't bleedin' got one!" he retorted.

I've had a ruff deal

31

Disappearing Dinosaurs

Learned men have theorised
When dinosaurs walked on the Earth,
Following global catastrophe,
There was suddenly a dearth
Of these strange colossal creatures
With very little brains.
What laid them low? The little we know,
Is in fossilised remains.
Their findings are debatable
Most blame the creeping ice,
The dinosaurs could not adapt
And paid the freezing price.
But reasons deeper - more profound
Explain their annihilation.
And I believe it's in the names
They were given at their creation.
While they were nibbling foliage
And danger lay ahead,
By the time they shouted, "Ichthyosaurus, look out!"
They were caught and killed stone dead.
When heading for a treacherous cliff,
"Hypsilophodon, get back!"
Took too long to shout and warn
And they were dead upon the track.
Their eventual disappearance
Just leaves me this to say,
Had they been called, Bill, Fred or Jim,
They'd be here to this day.

Dress Rehearsal

Seven! There should be eight.
Where's the reindeer?
Not you, Prancer - Rudolph!
At the toilet!
This is no time for reindeers to ....
Oh, he can't do up his poppers,
I knew we should have used Velcro.
Mary, don't do that, you're the mother of God.
What do you mean, you can't say Frankincense?
Everybody can say Frankincense,
It's in all the carols.
Oh, you're the one with the problem.
Who chose you? The student -
I might have known.
Angels over here, Angels, Angels
GET IN LINE THIS INSTANT!
No, you can't wear a shell suit.
Well, I don't care what your mother says,
MY angels are all white sheets and tinsel.
Because I'm a traditionalist, that's why.
What do you mean, Jesus's head has come off!
It was on when I left it. Everybody look for it,
We can't have a headless Son of Man.
You should have known it wasn't a football!
Go and ask the Janitor for some superglue.
Joseph - don't do that with the donkey.
No, you can't be a wise man - you're a shepherd.
BECAUSE I SAY SO!
Right, after 3 - sing! And I mean everybody! 1, 2, 3,
"Christmas is a time of peace and joy."

SHELL-SHOCKED

The Sergeant bristled angrily
Indignation in his stride.
"My men can't do it, your Majesty
We're a regiment with pride.
A honed and well-oiled fighting team
We're the best - we're not the dregs.
The Royal Horse and King's Own Men.
Shouldn't be ordered to mend eggs!"

The adamant King refused to yield
He wasn't hard boiled after all.
He felt in part responsible
Being the owner of the wall.
The soldiers tramped off angrily
They knew it was no joke.
They'd seen the hell of exploding shell
And they'd never tried fixing yolk!

These battle trained and hardened men
Reached the scene with trepidation
Where Humpty took his fatal fall
Was a scene of devastation.
So hard and eager though they tried
They reached the end of their tether.
Realising when it came to eggs
They couldn't get it together!

Granpa'

My Grandad's a museum
Folks should pay to come and see him.
In his Antique Roadshow suit
In which he seems to put
The treasures of the decades of his life.
He has medals from the war,
Can't remember what they're for.
And to whittle bits of wood
When he's feeling in the mood,
He has a finely honed and sharpened pocket knife.

He always speaks in clichés
No matter what he says,
Crying, "Turned out nice again
If it wasn't for the rain."
"What will be, will be", "That's life" and other copied phrases.
He's a walking almanac
With the twinges in his back
Predicting snow and sleet
As he hobbles down the street,
His huddled body trapped within his braces.

The worn hills in his bunnet
Fixed the way he's always done it
Bucking every fashion trend,
It's a battered, faithful friend
As it sits in Royal splendour on his pate.
He'll embarrass his "better half"
With his knotted, knitted scarf
Which he'll wear and then perspire
As he sits down by the fire
While spitting rapid rounds into the grate.

People never seem to mind
Him being grumpy, 'cos he's kind
Underneath his crusty front.
Still, he girns as is his wont
About his pension, or his wife, or feeling ill.
He is common yet unique
Giving strength while growing weak.
And you feel one dark filled day,
If he ever has to go away
He'll leave a space that's very hard to fill.

House Hunting

The couple said they were House Hunting.
Poor House.
Poor Defenceless House
What had it done to them?
Did they give it a fair chance
To run for its life
Before setting off in pursuit
And mowing it down
With schedules and mortgages?
Was it done humanely
Or did it suffer?
No doubt they will say they did it
To keep the prices stable.
Culling keeps the population down
And saves the green belt.
How long will it be
Before a group of concerned people
Form a society
To ban this cruel sport?

Jack The Yak

Jack the Yak bought a hobby book,
The answer to his prayers.
For there's not much for a Yak to do
High up in the Himalayas.

The book suggested dancing
He practised all the week.
But found he kept on falling
As he lived on a mountain peak.

There's no chance of being Nureyev
Or even worse, Wayne Sleep,
When every third step sideways
You fall 5,000 feet!

So bruised but not defeated
He turned another page
And read that home-made souvenirs
Were currently all the rage.

Out came the papier mâché
To make a Highland scene,
But tourists to a mountain top
Are few and far between.

Just the odd explorer came
But didn't want to know,
There's not much room for souvenirs
When your rucksack's full of snow.

Jack lost all his money
And got deeply into debt.
There's not a sadder Yak than Jack
In the whole of old Tibet.

The hobby book was close to hoof,
Try cooking, it advised.
And gave a secret recipe
For making home-made pies.

But though he hunted high and low,
Food never came to pass.
All he found to fill his pies
Were lumps of withered grass.

So battered, broke and hungry,
And wishing he was dead,
He did the one thing left to do
And ate the book instead!

JUST A PHASE

When it's 3am in the morning
And up and down the floor you pace
Your mother-in-law, who knows better than you,
Will take delight in saying to your face,
"It's just a phase."

When you've newly changed his nappies
And you're rushing for the train,
Just as you leave and lock the door,
He'll fill the blighter up again.
It's just a phase!

When you're checking out at Tesco's
And he's grabbing for the sweets
You console yourself as people glare
As on the floor his head he beats,
It's just a phase!

When he's going to a party
Dressed in all his finest clothes
It's then he falls in the sandpit
Or has some fun with the garden hose.
It's just a phase!

When you're due to attend a function
In your blouse of finest silk,
A last wee cuddle to say goodbye
And 'BURP' he covers you in milk!
It's just a phase!

As the years roll on and on
Every time he falls from grace,
Your mother-in-law, who knows better than you,
Will delight in telling you to your face,
"It's just a phase!"

Non-Stick Pans

Back to the Hardware shop, the woman went,
Very cross indeed.
"I've come about those non-stick pans,
The ones you guaranteed."
The puzzled manager shook his head
And took one from the shelf.
"We've never had a soul complain
Apart from your good self!
These pans are non-stick guaranteed.
They'll handle any chore.
Hardened lumps of grease and grime
Are gone for evermore."
The irate woman shook her fist.
"That's no use", she said.
"My little lad took your non-stick pan
And stuck it on his head!"

———————◆◆◆———————

O Sole Destroying Me-O

Ever since the World Cup
A host of epiglottii
Have warbled in the sad belief
They can sing like Pavarotti.
The Postman's La Donna Mobile
Can have the eyes tear-brimmed,
While the Milkman's Nessum Dorma
Would turn his semi-skimmed.
On an array of Yuppie stereos
Once humming to Dire Straits,
Carreras sings Caruso
Or La Traviata waits.
Karaoke's been superseded
Now every Tom or Dick or Harry
Can let his arias unleashed
And mutilate Volare.
When I'd overdosed on Placido
And my ears were opera-weary,
The cleaner came in - a Rugby fan
And she now thinks she's Dame Kiri!

I can singa likea da milkman

39

LONG MAY HE RAIN

When summer TV watchers
Tune in once again
They're becoming armchair experts
On the different types of rain.
There's cricket rain which seems to fall
From 10 o'clock to six
And heralds close analysis
Of the different types of drips.
Superlatives from Richie,
Analysis from Johnson.
Constant reruns of old games
As they wonder where the sun's gone.
Then "Oh, I say", There's tennis rain
Harder, yet more refined
Dripping discreetly on the covers
While Dan and Virginia combined
Wax lyrical on rain they've known
Throughout the passing time.
Does British rain match foreign rain
Or is it in decline?
There is snooty rain at Ascot
Tough rain for athletics
Earthy rain for Gardening Time,
It's really quite pathetic.
Why do we watch TV so much
And spend our time complaining?
Because we cannot go outside,
It's always blooming raining!

Old Hippies Never Die
(They Fade Just Like Their Jeans)

Worn like his Donovan records
Gone a whiter shade of pale
His thoughts on peace and happiness
Like himself are old and frail.
His hairband styled in Indian art
In place - though not now needed.
The flowing locks it held in place
Having long ago receded.
His children, Sky and Harmony
Have left him to his games
And are something in the city
Living under assumed names.
In his ageing hand-stitched lifestyle
Where he weaves his dreams of peace
The plants he grew in his garden
Confiscated by the police.
His wife stands in the kitchen
Making pots of rhubarb jam,
Sighing, "I cook, I wash, I hoover,
I bake - therefore I am."
Their flower-decked mini - now a shed
Where free range hens lay speckled eggs,
While home-made wine from an unknown vine
Is drunk down to the dregs.
The multi-coloured cares of life
Are nuts cracked with a mallet,
As ageing white and gathering dark
Are mixed up on the palette.

41

PETS

It was pets today
So I took my slug,
We'd been lifelong friends for days.
I called him Cedric
And we watched Neighbours
Together.
He was the best slug I ever had.
In his Swan Vestas matchbox
He was right at home
But Teacher screamed
And I dropped him.
The class ran out to find him
But accidentally
He was trodden on!
I buried him
Still in his matchbox
Then went home
To watch Neighbours Alone.
Next week it's hobbies
But I'm taking nothing.

◆◆◆

JOHN LENNON'S LEGACY

It was question three in a quiz game,
In some trivial pursuit.
Who was Mark Chapman
And what 'person' did he shoot?
Is that the fate of the famous?
Is that why they're taken out?
To be question three in a quiz game
Is that what it's all about?

Punch Up

Scenes at the seaside,
Horror, terror, shock!
Wouldn't be shown on TV
Till after 9 o'clock.
A man beats up his child then assaults his wife.
Policeman hurriedly summoned,
Is threatened with his life!
Thwack, thwack, thwack, thwack!
Policeman's beat.
Kids encourage perpetrator,
Think it is a treat.
Fratricide, homicide
And other cides beside.
Violence, murder, mayhem
Rising with the tide.
Supernatural goings on
Don't seem to phase the host,
It seems to raise his spirits
When he castigates a ghost!
A mob of noisy children
Who an hour ago were quiet,
Are on their feet and shouting as
He incites them near to riot.
Now Satanic practices!
The devil comes as well.
Is caught up in this mortal's schemes,
As he gives him merry hell.
Mr Punch shows no remorse
For all the people he hurt, he
Shouts, "That's the way to do it, folks!
Next show at 4.30!"

He does it just to keep his hand in you know.

RECESSED RHYMES

The harsh realities of life
Have cut through Fairyland like a knife
And rhymes that once were rich and blooming
Have suffered economic pruning.

No more the wolf shows his intent
To blow pig's house of strong cement.
Instead they have a little fox
And pig lives in a cardboard box.

While Goldilocks, that temptress fair
No longer tangles with 3 bears,
By chairs and beds no more obsessed
Their porridge has been repossessed.

There's no more well for Jack and Jill,
They haven't paid their water bill.
Brown paper still on fractured dome
The hospital's opted out on its own ....

And poor McDonald, ee ay o
His animals have had to go.
The choices facing him were stark,
His farm is now a Disney park.

The recession's hit them, one and all
The giant's only four foot tall.
While Jack, unable to find means
Has had to eat his magic beans.

Mother Goose, her gold all gone
Lays plastic eggs in from Hong Kong.
Their fantasy world is overspent,
A victim of the government.

SILVER TONGUED

The door creaked open - a shaft of light
Startled past into the night.
And there framed stood a figure vast,
'Twas Long John Silver, home at last.
Mrs Silver rose from the fire
Which she'd been stoking with her ire,
Mentally stabbing at the grate
Long since deprived of pieces of eight.
His warming slipper, like her ardour, cooled
Many times bitten, no longer fooled.
With tales of his voyages, he did regale her,
Which proved to be an abject failure.
He'd only been gone since half past two
With that reprobate sailor, Old Blind Pew.
She knew for certain he did then go
For a pint of ale at the Admiral Benbow
But the taste of one leads to a few
And it ended up with John blind, too.
She advanced - he framed the fire eclipsed
And a verbal broadside caught him midships.
A mass of righteous indignation
No pause for breath, no hesitation.
"You're a waste of space, my life's in ruins
When did you last bring me dubloons
Or pearls, or diamonds - Spanish gold?
My love like your slipper has gone cold.
There's nothing in this house to eat
Except a parrot with dandruff on his feet."
John paused for Polly to interject
But the bird was silent - she'd wrung his neck!
"He could speak 5 languages!", he cried.
"Well, why didn't he speak before he died!
I'm sick of this life, I'm sick of you.
They say love is blind and you love Old Pew."
"He's a mate o' mine and talking of which,
I left him lying in a ditch.
With mucky water up to his ear
Saying he didn't much like the beer."
He hopped off with alacrity
Saying, "I think I'll run away to sea."
As in pursuit with pan she plunged.

STAG NIGHT

Stag night, Brag night
Have a pint with the lads night
Don't think
Drink, drink
Tomorrow's distant, out of sight.

Stag night
Get tight
Drink him under the table.
Think of the aisle
That's the style
Don't think he's gonna be able!

Stag night
A drag night
Think of the things that he's missing.
More drink
Think think
Everyone starts reminiscing.

Stag night
Big fight
Glasses and fists are all flying
Black tie
Black eye
Bride and her mother are crying.

Stag night
Groom's plight
Fills his pals full of sorrow
Though sad
Can't be as bad
As he's going to feel tomorrow.

State Of Affairs

He sat in accounts and dreamed of her figure
She scribbled the minutes and watched the hours pass
Till sitting alone
In a small crowded café
They colluded in whispers
Together at last
Freedom's assumed
Like the names they were using
They lay in hotel rooms
And talked of their life
Swift stolen moments of bosoms and bedrooms
She thought of the future
He thought of his wife!
Their timetabled love
Fitting in with his journey
Embarrassed she lay
As he dressed and departed
Clinging to memories she hoped would sustain her
Through her wallpaper life
She would not be down-hearted
Alone on the train
He gazed from a window
Furtive and sad, he seemed a lot older
As the 5.32
Sped him home to his loved ones
To his reheated soup
And a slice of cold shoulder.

SUMMER MADNESS

When rainy summer skies relent
And reluctant shards of sun peep through
Do people stop to contemplate
Nature's wonders, admire a view?
No! These gourmatic lemmings run
To light their barbecue.

Rusting metal trays are filled
So dervish figures can cajole
With a year's supply of lighting fuel
Life from wizened lumps of coal
Which suddenly flare with cauldron heat
And singe their hair and eyebrows whole.

Lumps of meat are placed on sticks
Chicken wrapped in metal foil
Hamburgers hacked from frozen piles
Turned constantly so as not to spoil
While guests invited for the feast
Drink wine and leave him to his toil.

So fighting wasps and apathy
He hands his wares to those who scoff
Cinder black on the outer skin
While inside cold as a penguin's chuff
They chew, not realising salmonella is
But just a short way off.

He likes the rituals of the feast
Mastered them with little training
Sweats for hours over heated grill
Spattered with fat but not complaining
While everyone else has gone inside
Because it's started raining!

The Blue Peter Presenter's House

The Blue Peter Presenter's house is amazing
Fab, brill and utterly fantastic!
The windows are glazed sweetie wrappers
The front door is sticky backed plastic
The bath is made from used Coke cans
The remnants of some age-old appeal
While in it swim two little goldfish
Three ducks, a frog and a seal.
The wallpaper's compiled of old post stamps
Sent from all over the world
While the fridge is choc full of 'home bakes'
With stale fillings and edges all curled.
The carpet is home-made and comfy
Sewn together with thousands of tufts
From the hair of the Blue Peter doggy
Which did something special at Crufts.
The stairs are used for abseiling
While the garden is needing a mower
Like the present Blue Peter garden
It requires a new Percy Thrower.
The walls are draped with kids' paintings
And ornaments sent by Aunt Madge
And instead of paying the milkman
They give him a Blue Peter badge.
Life here is always uncertain
You can say it's never a bore
And the house next door is no better
It's one they made up before!

THE LEGEND

Alone on the midfield stage he stands
Hands on hips barking out commands.
Marshalling his troops to tackle with vim
Fight for the ball and give it to him.
So forty yard passes, he can launch
Hampered only by his paunch.
He tiptoes gently through the dirt
His credibility stretched out like his shirt.
For time has caught this ageing star,
He doesn't like to run too far.
No more the probing midfield rover,
A 10 yard run and his eyes mist over.
He palpitates and fights for breath,
An athlete who has diced with death.
But beware the upstart, gangling youth
Who mistakes his pained and gasping truth
His balding pate, his dragging feet,
As an ageing star who's easy meat.
For knowledge amassed in a long career
Comes to his aid when danger's near.
A trailing foot - a shoulder blade
And low the gangling youth is laid.
He takes the ball and parts with it,
The hands on knees he stops to spit
If skill and grace were measured in phlegm,
He's up there with the best of them.
The final whistle stops the game,
It terminates his hour of pain.
And now he shows his speed by far
By being first up to the bar.
He blossoms, nurtured by the beer
Regales them with his long career
How once when young and in his prime
He scored a goal from the half way line.
A rising star who never made the grade,
But sat and watched as others played
And who staggers home through a halcyon mist
Waving the hand fate never kissed.
He'll never make the Hall of Fame
But he's been a credit to the game.

THE LOCH NESS MONSTER APPRECIATION SOCIETY AGM

The aficionados gathered
In Drumnadrochit village hall
To air their views on such issues
As consumed and concerned them all
It was the monster who had summoned them
Chairman Angus rose to speak
On the latest sighting of Nessie
Saying, "I think it should be next week!"

"The tourist trade is tailing off
They're no arrivin' like they can
An' I've 10,000 plastic Nessies
Ah've just imported frae Japan!
Mah boardin' hoose is just nae fu'
Stale porridge lies in the dishes
We'll hae tae revive the monster myth
If ah'm tae survive life wae ma missus!"

They certainly give
me the hump!

Dougal rose to interject
Saying, "Ma mither's gettin' tired
O' swimmin' in yon freezin' loch
Last year, she near expired.
She might o' had a better chance
If it wasn't for the factor
She was draggin' a stovepipe frae the lum
An' three tyres frae oor tractor!"

The proprietor saw his profits
Like his whisky being drowned
Said, "Tell yer maw, we'll double her fee
And make it up to a pound."
Dougal's eyes lit up with glee
He said, "Throw in a patch,
There's a hole in mither's wet suit.
That should bring it up to scratch."

The postcards rights went to Old James
The franchise caused him glee
He's still a photo his brother had taken
In 1953.
The business of the meeting done,
They adjourned to toast the beast.
"To Nessie, may she always be
The founder o' the feast."

THE MEANING OF LIFE

A Mystic climbed the Himalayas
To meditate and say his prayers.
He communed with nature, bathed in dew
His thoughts were many, his needs were few.
His mission to find the meaning of Life
And gain relief from his nagging wife!
He languished there for many a year
Till lost in time he disappeared.
Shrouded in mist and mystery
His fame spread far across the sea.
A professor in London College
Felt he had to have this knowledge.
If he met this man - with some insistence
He could have the secret of life's existence.
He withdrew his savings - financed a plan,
To make his mission to find this man.
For years he travelled far and wide,
Had narrow escapes and almost died.
Beaten by bandits, bitten by snakes
Caught strange diseases, near drowned in lakes.
Till finally, with his money spent
In failing health and his clothes all rent
He found a cave high on a hill
The sight he saw made his blood run chill.
For there before him sat the Maharishi
Inert, immobile, a man at peace. He
Begged him, "Please, end all my strife.
Why stay up here - what's the meaning of Life?"
The Mystic raised a quizzical eye
And proceeded then to tell him why
Though he'd climbed the mountain long ago,
He'd stayed up there through rain and snow.
His words filled the learned man with shock.
He said, "My bum's stuck to this rock!"

THE OTHER SIDE OF THE MOUNTAIN

Hello, Mr Piper
Hello, Mrs Piper.
Welcome home. Had a good day at work?
Yes, thank you dear
I tootled there and here
Once I get my wind I never shirk.

Well, Mr Piper
Yes, Mrs Piper.
Did you manage to bring me something nice?
Last week you brought me frogs
Before that it was dogs
And for Christmas, it was just a plague of lice.

Well, Mrs Piper
Yes, Mr Piper
I was called over to Hamelin for some rats
But the people wouldn't pay
So another tune I'd play
And I tootled off with all their little brats.

You mean, Mr Piper!
That's right, Mrs Piper
200 kids are waiting at the door
You fool, we don't need them!
How are we going to feed them?
And washing all their clothes will make me sore.

You fool, Mr Piper
Why's that, Mrs Piper
How are we going to send them all to school?
It's all just a mess
And I'm sure the DHSS
Won't pay for them - they'll have some bloody rule.

We are ruined, Mr Piper
No, we're not, Mrs Piper
Yes, we are, Mr Piper, Mrs Piper cried.

Where There's A Will

"We are gathered here."

Survey the gathering vultures
Hooded, black and crocodile cried
Butter wouldn't melt in their conscience
Always pious when not pie-eyed
Graspers!

"To read the last Will and Testament."

Blood was thicker than Walter
Close relations but only in name
They lived just round the corner
But never ever came
To visit.

"Of Walter Albert Jones."

They covet his ceramic teapot
Have designs on all his clothes
Reminisce on half grey snapshots
Recognise their static pose
Skinflints.

"Suffice to say, he left all his worldly goods."

A solitary figure, I alone
Was devoted, tendered to his needs
My motivation, love for him
While theirs was avarice and greed
Mercenaries.

"To the local dog and cat home."

Silly old sod!

PASSING STRANGERS

Sitting on the top deck, gazing into space,
Beside you is a vacant seat, a convenient empty place.
When you notice in the bus queue, the passenger from hell,
Who is big and fat and sweaty and you know is going to smell!
Smoking like a chimney, exhaling poisonous cloud,
He pushes, as the bus draws up, in front of the waiting crowd.
As you hear his ominous footsteps come plodding up the stair,
You throw your bag on the empty seat in a measure of despair.
Then pretending you are sleeping, you glance out of one eye,
But he's standing by your shoulder saying, "Do you mind if I
Sit here pal? No? thanks a lot", he descends like a lead balloon,
And you're squashed against the window with an impending sense of gloom.
He regales you with his lifestyle, oblivious that he bores.
His garlic breath and beads of sweat leaking out of all his pores.
You cannot read your paper with your arms pinned by your side.
So getting up and leaping off, you terminate your ride.
Though you are miles away from home and you're going to miss your tea,
As he disappears in the distance, you ask yourself, "Why me?"

FOOLS GOLD

Where is the man inside the man,
Who used to run
For fun?
Imagined glories spurred him on
Swallowing -
His pride
Increasing his speed
For greed.
Altered the rules of the game
Extinguished the flame
Holding the gold
That dimmed and grew old.

A Visit To Ann Frank's House

A steep staircase
Leads to a bookcase
That hid their rooms
And barred their dreams
You hesitate
Before crossing through it
Somehow reluctant
To trespass on a private place
That should belong only to them.
The rooms are bare,
The windows covered
And the walls, still hung
With scraps of their living,
Seem to close in
Almost breathing
As if they wish to unburden
Their secrets.
The hopes, the longing
And the ultimate suffering
They bore silent witness to.
Downstairs the faces stare out
Ann, her parents, her family,
The people who helped them
Travel so near to freedom
Only to be betrayed
When the end was in sight.
Ordinary people
In extraordinary times
There is a lingering sadness
That goes with you
As you walk into the street
Which they could never do.

Batteries Not Included

The toys ground to an inevitable halt,
Three hours after the turkey died,
Batteries not included.
Dad passed out in front of the Queen,
His Christmas spirit satisfied,
Batteries not included.
Dorothy paused on The Yellow Brick Road,
The rainbow dipped in time,
Batteries not included.
Mother stood at the kitchen sink,
Sipping memories in wine,
Batteries not included.
The three wise men rest at the stable,
Their precious gifts to hand,
Batteries not included.
Yet Christmas still meanders on,
With a message deep across the land,
Batteries not included.

Circles

Knots in my stomach, sweat on my hands,
Violence - you know I abhor it.
But teacher said anyone making a mess
Or scratching the desk, would be for it!
I was drawing a circle, three quarters way round
It shot off - before I could stop.
I get the same compass every time,
The one that's loose at the top.
Perhaps if I asked, Jim'll Fix It.
Next time we have Geometry, please,
Could you fix a compass given to me
That draws 360 degrees.
Teacher descends, a scowl on his face,
His hand deals swift retribution.
Perhaps to get decent compasses,
We should have a revolution!

THE CREEPY CRECHE

There's something strange at Fortynine
A lady who looks like Frankenstein.
She's big and fat with a double chin
With a warty smile, she welcomes them in.

The mothers leave their tiny tots
Packed lunch in small black cooking pots
Kiss their little dears goodbye
And take off quickly into the sky.

A row of black nappies on the line
Little black broomsticks tied with twine
Her little charges create a din
As she anchors them with a safety pin.

Frogs leg yoghurt, she needs lots and lots
The supermarket sells her juice that clots
The strangest sight you've ever seen
Their milk is a lovely shade of green.

When they take a walk - all in a line
She goes in front, they fly behind.
Up and down on their leads they zoom
Like a bunch of fresh, pink faced balloons.

There's purple smoke comes from her fire
Wailing and howling from a deathly choir
I'm glad her house isn't next to mine
The lady who lives at Fortynine!

MOVING ON

The faces framed and smiling climbed the wall,
While fading, sad but slowly, from his life.
Empty spaces hung around his home
Left there by his loved but long-gone wife.
The time had come for moving on
To place his house in other hands.
To sign away his memories
And fold away his maps and plans.
Soon they'd come and take his world
In boxes to a special room.
Selling off what couldn't go
No choice in what to give to whom.
He didn't fit into this age
That passed the needy and the sick
He couldn't understand a world
Where watches didn't tick.

———◆◆◆———

DIVIDE AND CONQUER

"Let's take two apples,
And cut them both
In 4 pieces."
"What kind of apples?"
"It doesn't really matter!"
"Yes, it does.
If it's the green kind,
They give me
Stomach ache."
"But it's only ...."
"Only my health!
Are you trying to poison me?"
"The apples don't count."
"Yes, they do,
Because we're dividing them."
"They're hypothetical !"
"Well, I only like Cox's Pippins."
"Okay, okay.
Take two potatoes."

A HALTING SIGN

When the council in their infinite wisdom
Decide once again to dig up the road
There's one employee above all the others
Who has to bear the heaviest load
Some hidden hierarchy deems it is he
Who stands in the road for most of the time
And filters the traffic past red cones and workers
By constantly turning his red and green sign.

You see him standing at green on approaching
And, hoping to nick through, the old foot goes down
But he grins as he sees you speeding towards him
And just as you reach him, he turns his sign round
By some hidden sixth sense, he knows you are late
For a meeting, your margin of error is slight
And holds his sign red for what seems time eternal
As you grip the wheel and your knuckles go white.

But most galling of all is that while you are waiting
Stomach ulcers forming and air turning blue
The way that is barred remains silent and empty
No oncoming traffic ever seems to come through
When finally he wakes and in his humble opinion
The road is now safe for your car to proceed
You find you have stalled and you cannot get started
Life, like his pole, is twisted indeed.

———————◆◆◆———————

DEATH OF A DRY STANE DYKER

Stretching down the centuries
The dove-tailed walls.
Natural masterpieces
Of crafted stone.
Till the skills are ended,
At a dyke half mended
Scattered boulders wait
For a craftsman gone.
The gap in the wall
Stares out wistfully
Onto a world
Of barbed wire fences.

Two Way Stretch

The hand that fate had dealt to Jim,
Was poor in the extreme.
He plodded on, while others excelled,
Achieving - while he'd just dream.
He'd lost his job - last in first out,
No hint of compensation.
His wife had gone to pastures new,
And left him at the station.
He'd just been mugged - his wallet gone.
His car was repossessed.
His folks had packed and moved away,
Leaving no address!
As Jim stood on the local bridge,
Eyeing the black and flowing river.
Plucking courage to throw himself down
And end his trials forever.
"I'll be at peace!" Jim cried - and jumped,
Arms spread as he hurtled down.
"This noble gesture ends my span,
Who cares if I live or drown?"
But fate conspired to cheat on Jim,
Of compassion showing no traces.
Ornamental ironwork on the bridge
Had entangled in his braces.
And as he touched the coursing flow,
His braces went full stretch,
And flung him high back in the air,
The unfortunate yo-yo'd wretch.
Down he hurtled one more time,
But his braces took the strain
And stretching buttons to the limit
He bounced back up again!
Eventually dangling 'neath the bridge,
Jim said, "I've found out something!
I'm not a failure after all,
I've invented Bungee jumping!"

THE SCOTTISH CUP FINAL 1989

It was only a six yard pass back
Stevens failed to connect
Miller nipped in like a whippet
And rifled the ball in the net.

A current of green raised the terrace
The scarves and the flags were unfurled
While the blue at the other were burdened
With all the cares in the world.

On such moments are cup finals settled
And despite all the sweat and endeavour
There was no coming back from the depths of despair
The glitter had vanished forever.

Homeward we trod with half-masted scarves
Sunk between anguish and shame
Deaf ears brush off whispered clichés
When they tell us, "It's only a game!"

THE SANDS OF TIME

I came again to the postcard beach
Retracing steps on golden sand
Leaving water-filled footsteps where I walked
As the incessant sea ate up the land.
I drifted back on familiar sounds
To warm-remembered holidays
Where we left out sand boats to the waves
Grew up and went our separate ways.
Standing here I feel this place
Will survive the ravages of time
And our children will come to build castles anew
On the silvery sands where I once built mine.

THE OLD LADY LINGERS

She was old even then when our affair first started
On a grey windswept Saturday, Autumn 1959
Third Lanark played Hearts in a League Cup final
Bedecked in Red and White, the beaten team was mine.
But I was seduced by her towering terraces
The mass of humanity in one common band
Peopled rows of concrete fanning out skywards
The press room like a matchbox on top of the stand.
And here lie the memories that keep me returning
Soaring on high or plunged in despair
Clutching a programme and Evening Times Special
The drama, the tension, the teams and the players.
The orchestrated brilliance as Real hammered Eintracht
Jim Baxter's Scotland beating England again
Dunfermline's Cup glories, Rangers elegant heroes
Billy McNeil's header starting Jock's Parkhead reign.
The World Cup glories - and ignominies
Pre-Argentine Ally carving out his own niche
They led us to Germany, Mexico and Spain,
Jim Holton, Joe Jordan and Kenny Dalglish
John Grieg's strike that made Italy shudder
Before we bowed out leaving England to win.
The Centenary Cup Final with Rangers and Celtic
And Tom Forsyth's six incher that took hours to go in.
Now old, aged and ravaged, the facade is crumbling
The cracks are appearing as the legend lives on.
Will she survive and be given a facelift
Or die, condemned like a prisoner at dawn?
Replaced by an all seated multi-purpose stadia
Custom built with comfort and new dreams on parade
But I can't take my son and show him the places
Where I stood as a boy and saw history made.

THE NATIVITY

Joseph.
This year I gotta be Joseph!
My dressing gown's ironed
My tea towel is smart,
I know I'll really look the part
Of Joseph.
Being the Innkeeper is OK
But he just tells them, "Go away."
That's not much of a part to play.
I gotta be Joseph.
The wise men they all dress up rich.
That's alright but there's a hitch.
They don't come on till near the end,
Following a star, give the knees a bend,
Talk about Herod, have a good moan,
Leave a few presents then hurry off home.
Kings for a moment, but then they are gone.
I gotta be Joseph.
The same with the Shepherds who've woken from sleep
They just wander in and leave a few sheep,
Have a look at the baby
Then back to the hills.
Hardly a part to exhibit my skills
But Joseph,
Yes, that's the part
He's on from the start.

PLANET SWEET

I'd like to offer up a prayer
For a disappearing ozone layer.
Let us spray.
The million little things that died
Covered in insecticide
The blackened leaves that curl in pain,
Bowing down to acid rain,
The cars that billow out their fumes,
The strangled air in smoke-filled rooms.
The toxic waste that's oozing in
Starving the rivers of oxygen.
The creeping drought in man-made dust.
We close our eyes and ears and just,
Say "Let us spray."

The Thrift Shop

A small lonely teddy bear,
One-eyed and sad.
Sits on a shelf dreaming
Of the life he once had.
Lying next to a suit
That is well past its prime
It once shone at weddings
Now it's just left to shine.
Old books, scratchy records,
Of now faded stars
Half-filled colouring in books
Bashed 3-wheeled cars.
Crockery, cutlery, chipped china, glass.
The flotsam and jetsam of everyone's past.
Side by side in the thrift shop
They lie sad and alone
Always hoping some stranger
Will give them a home.

The Noble Art

Puff-faced, near brain dead, and crouched like a rag doll
The pugilist grunts a blood smeared cough,
Face red-lined like an old AA road map,
Seen more canvas than Vincent van Gogh.
Jellied legs wobble, unable to hold him,
Staggering ringside - the end of round 10.
From a black battered brow, sweat pours profusely
His instincts cry out he is nearing the end.
Nose spread like butter on a face with glazed eyes,
Gloved fists hang limply down by his side.
The crowd baying loudly, filled with a blood lust,
Seated and safe they are wanting his hide.
The triumphant fanfare - the monogrammed robe,
The spangled shorts and the platitude,
Seem a long time ago - now faded and tarnished,
By the sweat and the gore - and the being booed.
From hidden reserves an effort is summoned,
Fat lipped comments spit into the mike,
"I fink I've done well to come out the winner,
You should see wot the 'uvver bloke's like!"

PLAYING "IMAGINE"

I played the record
And I bought the dream
Wanting.
The voice that chilled
So abruptly stilled
Haunting.
The message clear
For us all to hear
Taunting.
Is it too naive
Or can we still believe?
Daunting.

———————◆◆◆———————

COOKERY CARDS

The cards arrived in shiny packs
Family meals and tasty snacks.
Puddings, soups, fresh bread and cakes,
With stars for ease and cost it takes
To conjure a gastronomic treat
And give it to my friends to eat.
The ingredients listed to put in it,
The time to give it - to the minute
I follow exactly and it's incredible
The end result tastes quite inedible!

"These cookery cards taste horrible"

66

POETIC JUSTICE

Inspired by a magazine
That published his first ditty,
He traded all his worldly goods
For a garret in the city.
He grew a little goatee beard,
Went to Oxfam for his clothes,
Wore shades and haunted jazz clubs,
As he suffered for his prose.
He bought a little bookcase
Which he filled with pseudy books.
Not purchased for their contents
But their tombed and dusty looks.
He wrestled with his metre,
He wrestled with his rhyme,
And he wrestled with his girlfriend
Because it helped to pass the time.
He produced his tortured verses
Torn from his very soul,
As he warmed his cooling talent
On a lonely lump of coal.
But then the dread occurrence
Which aspiring poets dread
He managed to sell a poem,
Which blew apart his cred.
From there his talent went downhill,
So fast he couldn't stop. He
Sold his flat, shaved off his beard
And now writes ad man's copy.

EXPERTS

Experts design and build aeroplanes,
They say will last forever.
Then turn up at the crash site,
To tell you why they never.

Experts appear on television
As you are dining with your wife
And tell you what is on your plate
Will take 10 years off your life!

Fashion experts pontificate
On what's worn by the nation
Crippling shoes and skirts so tight,
They cut one's circulation.

Experts planned our skylines
Concrete rings of motorway.
They systemise our football teams
Taking flair out of their play.

Experts built Chernobyl
As well as the Titanic.
If the cry goes up, "Call experts in"
Then that's the time to panic.

How do I know about them?
I always keep alert.
I've studied them closely, and indeed
I'm something of an expert.

THE JANITOR

He patrolled the playground, broom in hand.
Not scared to give a reprimand,
To wayward pupils nearing riot.
Once glance from him - and all was quiet.
His thin moustache and flattened hair,
His rasping voice designed to scare.
Always ready to restrain
Those who threatened his domain.
His threshold low to undue noise.
A loathing deep for girls and boys.
A happier place he thought, no doubt,
If he could keep the pupils out!
Years later - walking in the street,
He and I just chanced to meet.
Old and frail, and out of breath
But still he scared me half to death.

DOG-GONE

There's a phantom dog in the city.
He never can be found
We only know he's been here,
By the messages left around.

No one ever admits it
No one cleans it up.
But everybody steps right in
This mess of a miscreant pup.

It always seems to happen
Whenever you buy new shoes.
It squelches over the edges,
And packs hard into the grooves!

No matter how hard you scrape them,
Along the pavement side.
The smell goes with you all the day,
Like something nasty died!

Joggers, walkers, victims all,
Shout, "It's a disgrace"
Somewhere sits the phantom pooch,
With a smirk across his face.

Instant Catherine Cookson

The local Squire, with loins afire,
Seduces local maid.
While his petulant wife, bored with life,
To the stables has essayed.
Where the stable hand flexes muscles grand
On a body tanned and slim.
Who would suspect, like an architect,
She has designs on him?
Then the wayward son, who'd been on the run,
Returns to claim his cash.
But his dad, the Squire, calls him a liar
And his windfall hopes are dashed.
So the errant heir, without a care
Pulls a gun from his apparel,
Crying, "You heartless swine, that cash was mine!"
He lets him have both barrels.
The poor old Squire, does thus expire,
As the stable lad rushes in,
And just for fun, the lying son
Tells the whole world it was him.
The false accused, hurt and bemused
Escapes the clutches of the law
And disappears for several years
To a life we know not of.
The grieving spouse, then leaves the house
Showing another of her facets
When poverty beckons, it's time she reckons
To transfer all her assets.
To the welcome charms of a soldier's arms
With a pension from the army.
But his military bearing, strict uncaring,
Eventually drives her barmy.
When the Great War comes, the drunken son,
Enlists, prompted by white feather,
And in No Man's Land meets the stable hand
And they learn to fight together.
Claimed by metal ball, he confesses all
And the evidence is produced.
The lad is free and returning he,
Marries the maid the Squire seduced.

NOSTRIL DAMN US

The plastic surgeon took his knife
And into his hands his client's life.
"Hold on tight, and here we go,
Mr ...er?" "Pinnochio!"

"A cosmetic cut, but listen to me
Your nose has perfect symmetry."
A tear welled up in Pinnochio's eye
"It has - until I tell a lie!

For one small Yes when I mean No
Is occasion for my nose to grow.
A beer with the boys, an occasional fling,
Are out - I can't control the thing.

For on returning to my house
I'm third-degree'd by my sweet spouse.
Whatever I say just doesn't affect her
It's her personal in-built lie detector."

The surgeon said, "Well, you're in luck,
I'll peg it with a nip and tuck
I'll stitch it up to keep it stable
And to live a high life you'll be able."

But though the surgeon plied his skill
Pinnochio's nose would not sit still.
The finished job made the doctors wince.
Resembling half a pound of mince.

As Pinnoch' recovered in the hospice,
He asked about his new proboscis.
"Perfect", the manic medic said, "A treat!"
Then cried as his nose shot out three feet!

FINGERS

God in his infinite wisdom
Didn't stop long to linger
And we marvel at his genius
When he made for us - the finger.
For no matter the size of the human
The fact of the matter is clear
When he wants us to poke out the wax bits,
It fits exactly into our ear.
And what is more interesting,
How it happens, nobody knows.
The same finger fits into your nostril
When you need a good pick at your nose.

IDEAL HOMES

Stretching skyward,
Concrete fingers
Filling pockets,
Not fulfilling dreams.
Crumbling slowly,
Sightless windows
Stare out sadly
On their housing schemes.
Only a few
Are left to mourn them.
Life has left them
Moving on.
Awards they gained
Buried beneath them
Those who gave them life
Have gone.

IMPERSONAL STEREOS

Walking along the street,
Peep, peep, peep.
A headful of noise,
Peep, peep, peep.
Oblivious to his environment,
Peep, peep, peep.
Especially a charging juggernaut,
Peep, peep, peep.
Thundering down the road,
Peep, peep, peep.
Just as he launches across,
Peep, peep, peep.
The music reaches a crescendo,
Peep, peep, SPLAT!

———————◆◆◆———————

THE EVERLY BROTHERS - '89

They came in their hordes to see them
Seeking a second hand thrill.
Crowding into the theatre,
To have their Don and Phil.
Many were past their sell-by date
But fresh with their memories.
Weightier now, yet poignant,
The legends appeared on the stage.
Their voices still held all the magic
That moved us all to tears
The audience were trapped in a time warp
As they sang away the years.
Then all too soon it was over,
The cats had savoured the cream
And returned to their worn-out albums
To dream, dream, dream.

Primary Colours

I took a big blob of green.
I like green.
And a big bristly brush,
That went squidge, squidgety, squidge.
It looked great on the paper,
All green and spattered.
Then I needed red,
For a head.
But I had none!
So I took black,
I didn't think it mattered.
The black all ran
Into the green
And turned it dirty brown!
The streaks that had all run down
I made into legs,
And a tail.
Miss came along and said,
"Tell me about your painting."
So I said it was a horse
She said, "Of course, of course.
I'll put it on display,
Right away."
But she hung it upside down!

Come Dancing

He the penguin
She the ostrich
Dancing like clingfilm
To long ago tunes.
Mothball presenters
From a black and white era
Spout forth their clichés
In 625 lines.
Perpetually smiling
These clockwork virtuosos
Give a brylcreamed performance
Without any faults.
Perpetual motion
In very strict tempo
Waiting for Victor
To play the Last Waltz.

Packed Lunch

Packed lunch was cheese today.
"So what", I hear you say.
Let me tell you, every lunch
All I get is cheese to munch ....
While other kids with goodies fed are,
I am stuck with lumps of cheddar.
Opening the lid, I'm praying "Please,
Don't let today's packed lunch be cheese."
But there it is all shining red,
Stuck between two bits of bread.
The other kids have meat and biscuit.
My Mum though, just won't risk it.
She says I need my vitamin C's,
And it's all there in lumps of cheese.
I don't know why she is so wary,
I think she has shares in a dairy.
I try to swap, but folks just scoff.
They know when they are better off!
I'm doomed. I'll never be a winner.
The alternative is to have school dinner!

Out Of Control

The cowboys rode into Coronation Street
Granny woke up - and wondered why.
Followed by lions eating Wildebeests
Under an African sky.
Had she missed a nuance of the plot,
Then it dawned on the poor old soul,
She's dozed, and given Dad the chance
To commandeer the remote control.

The family grown beyond command
Giving him feelings - deep - inferior.
By using control of the new TV
He reasserts his sense - superior.
His channel hopping, low attention span,
His zapping - drives her round the bend.
She reflects on happier TV Times
When she watched programmes to the end.

Valentines

14th February,
Here at last.
Out of bed
Clothes on fast.
Here he comes
Down the street.
The loyal postman
On his beat.
Heaps of cards
Coming my way,
Poems and flowers
Hooray, hooray!
Heart is sinking,
Face aghast.
Not one card
He's walked right past!
Rush out the door
Grab his lapel
"Where's my cards?"
He just says, "Well!
There's none for you."
"Oh", I say.
I hide a tear
And drift away.
Don't go to school
Can't face my chums.
Consumed by grief
The second post comes
At last, at last
Just one card came
It's from my Granny
IT'S NOT THE SAME!

THE ADJUDICATOR

We thought we were brilliant
He said we were naff.
We thought we were winners
He said, "Don't make me
laugh!"
Our lighting was tasteful
He said it was poor.
We thought it was funny
He said it was dour.
We spoke with distinction
He said he'd to strain.
Our pace was just perfect
He said we went like a train.
Our timing was perfect
He said we were late.
He slagged off our costumes
We thought they were great.
He slammed us in public
We sat there and fumed.
Our play was so dead
It was needing exhumed.
We saw him in private
To attack him we're free.
He said, "What did you think
then?"
"Well, we all quite agree."
He walks from the hall
He now is our enemy.
It doesn't really matter
What does he know, anyway!

TOMORROW IS

Tomorrow is the poem
That I didn't write today.
Honed in perfect craftsmanship,
A gem in every way.
Tomorrow is my children,
Growing tall and strong,
Finding purpose in the world,
A niche where they belong.
Tomorrow is the harvest
Of the seeds we sow today,
A gradual understanding
Of the price we have to pay.
Tomorrow is a different world
A changing attitude.
A dawning realisation
Of what we had was good.
Tomorrow is the old songs
Sung to newer tunes
And caring politicians
Without hot air speech balloons.
Tomorrow is a brotherhood
Of friends across the world.
Where flags of every nation
Together are unfurled.
Tomorrow's always out of reach
It's just a day away
But we can reach and touch it
By what we dream today.